I0190808

The
Poetry
of

Food

&

Drink

John Siwicki

1

Copyright © 2006 John B Slaby. All rights reserved.
No part of this publication may be reproduced, stored in a retrieval
system, or transmitted, in any form or by any means, electronic,
mechanical, photocopying, recording, or otherwise,
without written permission of the author.

ISBN 0-9774118-1-8

For Library of Congress Cataloging-in-Publication Data
please contact publisher

Poetic Art Published by:

SLABYPRESS
W25952 State Road 95
Arcadia, WI 54612

Order online at:
www.slabypress.com

Cover design and graphics by JBS

For information contact:
Slabypress

Poetry for...

The Connoisseur!

John Siwicki

Poems of Food & Drink

Poems of Food & Drink

Judgement

Appearance, what one sees
Hue, color, helpful light
Intensity of red and white

Age adds to the flavor
Maturity, growth, seasons pass
Soil, place, garden or path

Aroma, from dawn to dusk
Character, personality, alive
Kept in oak, sweet old wood

Taste, flavor, every time new
Sweetness, dry, sparkling
Persistent, well-balanced

Sound, a one-note concert
Pleasing to the ear
Crystal held in hand

Personality no longer hidden
Eye to eye contact
Our minds taste wine

Home

Ideal climate, vines thrive
Weather a worry to survive
In this season, stay alive

Summer the key, not too hot
Rainfall, but not a lot
Dangerous wind and cold

Well-drained soil
Stones absorb heat
Old world, new world threat

Slopes, flat land variation
Facing north, looking south
Higher ground, steep mountains

Ideal location with a view
Cultivation, hard-looking hands
Coastal beach, vineyard grand

Hot, humid, warm ripe fruit
Sweetness to excess, ice-wine
Dessert lusciously enjoyed

Buds emerge, then come flowers
Vines pruned twice each year
Color change, harvest autumn

Vines cry tears of joy
Thousands yield fruit

Into the bottles the sap of youth

Name

What is in a name?
Aren't they all the same?
Perfume, full of body

Cabernet, Sauvignon, Chardonnay
Gewürztraminer, Blanc, Gamay
Merlot, Pinot Noir, Riesling

Shiraz, Zinfandel, Semillon
Colombard, Muscat, Barrolo
Sangiovese, Chianti, Sylvanev

France, Italy and Spain
California, North America
South American wine for two

Australia, Japan, China, Africa
England, Wales, wine identity
Looking for some growing clue

Corked in a very good year
Sold for a high price

With best friends we share...

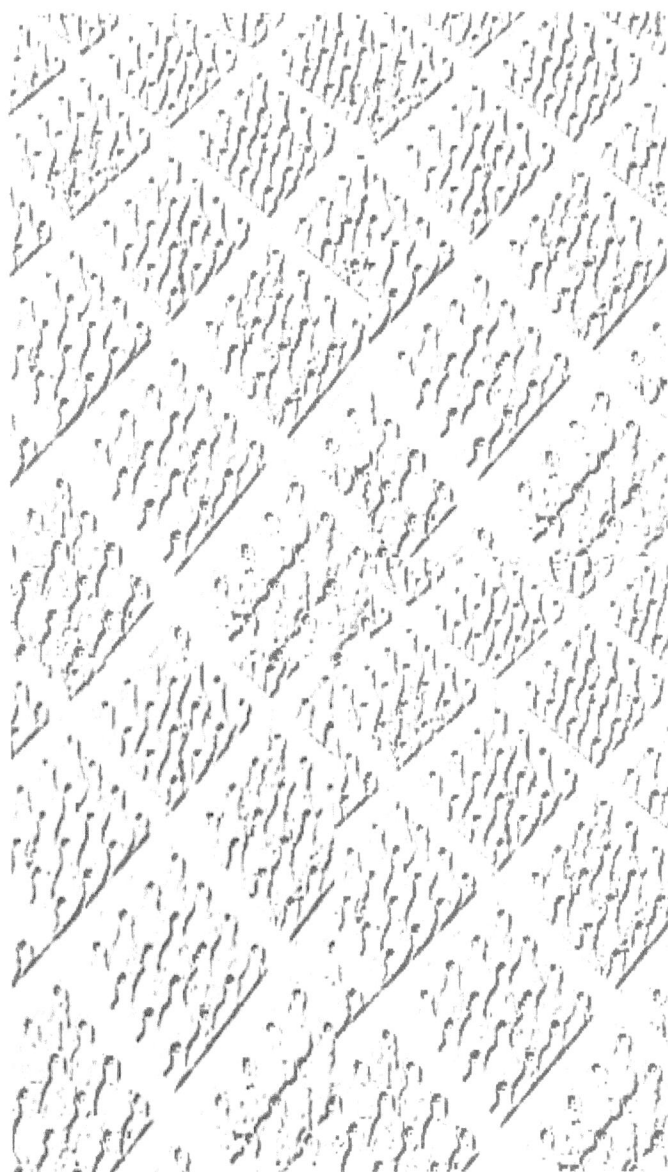

Village of Wine

Origin and style
Laws that control
Culture and climate change

Scenic old roads to enter
Roof tops, bell towers...
Cobble stone roads go below

Tramping footsteps heard
Skyline flying above
Counting one by one

Pomerol, St. Emilion Sauternes
Barriques mature and blend
Clairet the legacy we tend

Dijon, Lyon widespread fame
Demand grows, we hear the song
Where grower and merchant belong

Row after row I see
Estate of living green
Mountains, shadow, dream

Wagons, baskets, grapes
Bottles of spice, prolific
Lighted candle-wick

Together this romance we enjoy
Madeira, the people tread
We fortify and blend

Tawny, ruby, vintage
In this glass of three
Aged, tasted, then we agree

Sercial, verdelno, Bual, Malmsey
Light and dry, rich and sweet
On the stamp, burned with heat

Bottle design, shapes divine
Distinct label, showcase wine
Local food, modest and fine

Smoky Barolo, Asti we hail
In the theater, the audience
On the stage, blossom and yield

Left damp and then to cool
Rhine, sharp, sweet, strong
Bottles tall like forests

Napa, Sonoma, Russian River Valley
Zinfandel, rich, ripe and balanced
Worldwide for the heart fine

Night harvest, harsh white fruit
Soft red grape, Dutch date
South African landscape taste

Local conditions an advantage
The ceremony begins
Hundred year Eden Valley shiraz

Barrels stacked, round checked board
Barossa Valley, mountains and lakes
Seasons long, seasons cool

All here for us to absorb
Generations of family

Drink, toast, and cheer...

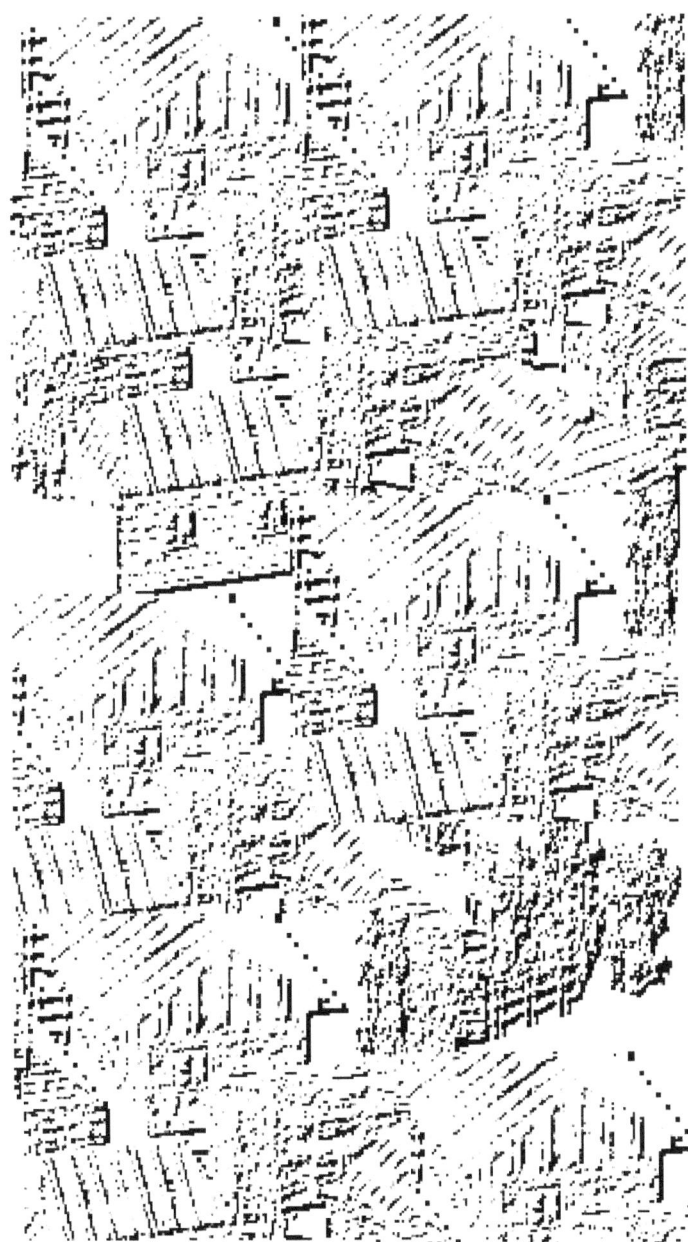

Vessel

First carried empty, then we harvest
Labor by hand, choose from sight
Tradition followed, time is tight

Sediment, fermentation the next step
Temperature, important and exact
Transported, arrive in tone provision

Crushed, extraction of flavor
Twice run from pressing
Falling bright, a filter bite

Bottled or into a cask to age
Sampling maturity and progress
Everyday wine, special wine

Into the cellars to wait
Years pass, value and desire
Price of happiness, warm to a fire

Oak rolling but motionless
Made by the master's hand
Character imparts, unbroken grain

Glass of color on the shelf to choose
Aeration, agitation gently done
Sealed with a cork stopper

Easily removed with a twist
Halfway up the bowl to the rim

Swirl, sniff, release and taste...

Flavor Trail

Many paths to follow
Taste, aroma, pleasure
Fruit fills the room

Wermut, Cinzano, Martini
Senses, sight, smell and taste
No scent intrusive or harsh

Meaningful clues conceal decay
Puzzle unlocked, treasure found
A hearty food and meal

Sediment and nature's light
Bright tone, legs and tears
The right glass for my bouquet

Whorl, then one deep sniff
Crisp, fruity, tannins zeal
Quality lingers long

Bananas, peas, black pepper
Toast, peach, apricot
Honey, nuts, lemons

Ideal balance and anatomy
Classic stoneware size and shape
My label, object made for me

Intrigued by the sight
Overwhelmed by the taste

Enchanted by the heart

Accord

Complement, balance, consideration
Overpower, weak, negotiation
Match the food, seek advice

Plate of bitter green, vinegar lemon
White Blanc, acidic suit
Sauce or fish, oak-aged Chardonnay

Texture saved from drowning
Clarify your subtle perfume
Rich and fruity wine

Follow and observe the golden rule
Together launch the team
Argue, then decide yourself

Fresh harvest, food and wine
A deal made, bottled, sold
Taken home to be enjoyed

Shared with all at the table
Talk, laugh and cry...

Happiness at every meal!

Home Grown

Tropic of Cancer, Tropic of Capricorn
Encircling the globe unseen
Hot and humid grows the bean

Arabica, Robusta choose from two
Arabica for the gourmet
Robusta for the rest of the fray

Our plants we cultivate
Hard work all day in the field
Good weather and season yield

Sensitive to all around
Enhance the flavor, special ground
Up in the clouds it grows

Blends are mixed for new flavor
Imagination song for life
With our friends we savor

The aroma drifts ether
Now under it's commanding rule

Both wise man and fool

23

Legend

Long fortunate history in short
Animals frolic in the court

Dark red berries on uxorious leaves
The goat herder as well did too...

Feeling stimulated, then renewed
Brought some for others to view

To a monk, a portion he did endow
This dark, red berry divaricate

Let fall into a boiling massive pot
A tipple of this dark bitter flux

Soon an uncanny, wonderful effect
Everyone, all awake without a wink

This is a miracle they proclaimed
Wonder rose from where it came

Fruity red cherries without a name
Beans roasted over open fires

Crushed and boiled in water
Then we drink this muddy mire

Criticized, called the devil's draft
Ban this beverage, we all think

Blessed by the Pope in ink instead
Coffee houses appeared everywhere

Tidings parted, covering a wide range
Beginning a springboard for change

Off to America, carried by the French
One plant becoming many

One cup costs merely a penny

Fragrant Compass

The world it found, now widespread
Earlier days of legends tell
Medicine, power, stimulation

Europe, then America traded
Growing markets, taxed at ports
Dealers, scientists, transplant beans

Plantations grow, workers live
Sailing the Mediterranean Sea
Along side tobacco and tea

Merchandise from known lands
Cafes open in Italian towns
First forbidden, then gossip abounds

Growing tall, success assured
Rough round table at the counter
Chit chat, eye to eye encounter

Warm dark wood, velvet amber lights
Tradition, invention, habitual
Pictuesque cafe, illustrations, sites

Linnaeus

Rubiacee, species of flowers
Subtropical, measure star and hour
Wild plant with healing power

Within the plantation cultivate
Stage of growth, then a tower
Dark red berry, bitter sour

Esocarpo cherry, sugary sweet
Outside golden yellow wheat
A silvery film covers the meat

White clusters of flowers neat
Rising from the rich peat
Assisted by the tropical heat

Coffee grown three-quarter-three
Plantation on the horizon I see
Watching sunsets filled with glee

Gather berries on my knee
Send them across the sea
A cheerful drink we all agree

Planted in favorable soil to thrive
Sensitive, but still they survive
Celebrate, the drink has arrived

Shaded nurseries to stay alive
No yield until year four or five
Flock to cafes, bees to a hive

Harvest with rakes or a hand
Our gift from the rich, rich land
Around the world, many brands

Held in the palm
Carried in baskets
Filled to the brim

Roasted a bit, then ground
Brewed for taste and flavor
An unforgettable aroma entices

A morning ceremony for many
Some throughout the day
A cup or two for a boost

Help me make it through the day
After lunch or dinner
Together all alone

Grind some beans, boil the water
Not so hard or long, make haste

On my tongue, enjoy the taste

29

Land of Spice

Roaming the trade routes, camels many
All loaded heavy with swollen pouches
Bringing merchandise from the east

A golden road, calendar and years
Pirates there awaken fears
Caravans venture with their wares

Soon by ship the merchant's guest
Exotic mysteries, no longer test
The unknown drink gated west

First the name was cha
Ancient knowledge decree
In the west known as tea

Ramusio traveled east and wrote
He served on the council of ten
He and others were powerful men

A Persian merchant told
The story of tea and cure
From then no stopping the lure

A missionary went to China
To spread the word of love
He found tea a gift from above

There he lived for 28 years
Learned customs, language, writing
Knowledge of tea graced his ear

Ships built especially for trade
Carrying goods and tea
On every trade route, it would be

The Sir Lancelot and Cutty Sark
Well-built famous clippers
Fast-sailing wave rippers

To London and America
Build the three mast
Oceans were no longer vast

It may be true or just a yarn
Once a great tea race in 1866
This is when it took place

From China to London
All carried cargoes of tea
Waiting, a prize and a victory

Wind-filling canvas aloft
Spectators agape, who was ahead
Clipper Aerial won, it is said

Steam power replaced the sail
Suez Canal, a new hasty way
Clippers met the end of their day

From one small planet
Around the world came
The drink with a new name

Wild Plant

Evergreen tall, kept small
To harvest tea for drink
Leaves fresh cultivated by hand

Tea plants from Camellia Sinensis
Process changes the type
Black, green, white, yellow, and red

Breakfast, lemon or milk
Earl Grey, English Prime Minister
Famous for his formula of tea

Twinings, Jacksons, Darjeeling
Mountains of India
Grow some fine teas

White tea the rarest one
Silver weedles, water sprite
Only a few times a year

Black Dragon, mellow and subtle
Burgundy wine, cherry shine
Smoky pine, orchid sweet and rich

Dragon well, green and mile
A most natural flower
Cure all drink for long health

All have a rich aroma
Evaporating into the air
Fragrance once it's named

Legends of monkey tea so high
They brought baskets of leaves
Only they could pick the trees

Demand increases, always more
All kinds of accessories I see
The power of, The John Company

English tax levied on the colonies
Boston harbor remembered today
St. Louis fair, ice tea a new way

Samples given away for free
Silk bags put into hot water
Mr. Lipton flo-thru tea

Chit chat, relax in the afternoon
This pleasure no crime
A moment now called tea time

6000 years old ?

Hanging side by side this pair
Slate dug from the earth
With its inscription shown
The evidence then read

Imagine the milling modulation
Listen to emmer being ground
Brewing the divine ancient drink
Life and the color of the sun

Most important, clean clear water
Loads of grain, barley, and malt
Between two rivers, Sumaria lay
Tigris, Euphrates, invention, chance

An epic story called Gilgamesh
Passed on to generations down
One story about Enkidu man
How he tested his strength

Gilgamesh gave him food
Then to drink the beer
Enkidu's life never the same
Enkidu a human being became

Household Art

So then it was mastered
The art of brewing beer
From emmer, barley, and grain
Exported to Egypt and far away

A daily ration for everyone
What your position allowed
As much as five liters a day
Exchange goods, none had to pay

If sold for silver or gold
The punishment was death
Poor quality not allowed
Into the river to be drowned

Greeks continued the brew
Romans chose wine
Not the barbarian drink beer
So on German soil, it did happen

Hallstatt time, amphora found
Kalewala verses, drink for mortals
Baking bread, brewing beer
From Edda we see and hear

The Monks

Long fast and frugal meal
A drink to satisfy
These monks would imbibe
More and more, they would brew
So much they could not drink
One day, an idea that was new
This drink we can share

Permission and right to sell
Quality, popularity and care
Monastery pubs, purveyors of beer
From over the land the people came
Soon burgeoning forms did the same
The monks pay no tax on their beer
We sovereigns do decree
No more monastery beer for free

Brewing art and legacy left
With hops the flavor made
Today the legend remains
King Gambrinus has taken credit
Because of where the monasteries lay
Beer's patron saint, he is still today

Grut

Herbs collected to add flavor
Important enough to have license
One brew master, special mixture

Some herbs were poison to man
Others made one see beyond
Oak bark, wormwood, caraway

Soon gone and hops chosen
Kept longer and more stable
Reliability and Purity law enforced

Use only malt, hops and water
Any other ingredient one adds
Will cause penalty, body and chattels

Growth and brewing centers grew
Financial reward and export begun
Friedrich the Great, drinking buddies

Modern time saw enormous change
Steam engines and cooling machines
Brewing all and every season

Steam beer it is called by name
New train line, two single barrels
So the drink spread its fame

Louis Pasteur's fantastic work
Micro organisms, micro breweries
Pasteurization, knowledge we know

Yeast culture and fermentation
Mr. Christian Hansen we thank you
Well-improved and best of taste

Prices too high, the people wail
For this we battle and rebel
Tap a keg, there are stories to tell

Brandy Trader

Spirit of wine, ancient time
Antiseptic, anesthetic, burnt fine
Grapes, blackberries or apricots
To transport a copious measure
 Inured a number of casks
An idea the Dutch Trader had
Out came the water on land
Casks loaded to stand
Then the cargo sailed to sea
After landing the ship
Water of an equal amount
The Dutch Trader did pour
Now a famous and popular drink
Cognac, Armagnac, Napoleon
One can judge, eye in a wink
Letters known to us all
VSOP, five years in wood
Napoleon at least four
Brandy made from wine
Sweet, bitter and smooth
 Hors D'age-time unknown
 Personal passion, from a vine

Whisky Man

Versions from east to west
Of the forty, which is best
Discovery from within the tribe

"Aqua Vitae" then "Uisque Baugh"
Suddenly appearing our whisky
A remedy to cure the sick

In Scotland it was widespread
Ireland as well can consume
Rye, barley and oats

Every class, titled to peasant
Soon to the underground
A secret plaque they found

English whisky, returned power
Scotland taxes, friendships sour
Then hatred every day and hour

Aeneas Coffey perfected distilling
Machines increase production
Spread until now without interruption

Spelled with or without an (e)
But for the finest taste
You'll buy the double wood

Nothing I've tasted since or before
And neither have been a whisky man

A bit over ice, but don't drink more

Smooth as white silk

Said to be the perfect bond
Healthy for bones as well
Natural from birth and good

Smooth and pours like silk
Basic color of all and everything
Babies stop crying, begin to sing

Butter, bread, chocolate ice cream
Perhaps a warm glass before bed
Through the night, a pleasant dream

Alone or with a hearty meal
Sometimes in coffee or in tea
Been around as long as the wheel

Frozen, made into a milkshake
Ordered with a hamburger & fries
An ingredient when we bake

There it sits on the table
A tall, clear, cold glass
History, legend and fable...

Juiced

Long ago-crushed by feet
Years past, smashed by hand
Now made by machine and heat
Choose your favorite fruit
It only takes a minute to make
And may satisfy your sweet tooth

Apple, orange, and grape are a few
Some I've never tried
One glass a day or perhaps two
At breakfast, lunch time too
A party, picnic fun
High school prom, spike the punch

Mixed drink cocktail
Quick hangover cure
Tropical fruit, wind in the sail
Hanging in and from the trees
Waiting to grow ripe
Picked ready to freeze

Frozen ice concentrate
Measure water and add
Lonely juice, no one can hate

Secret Formula

Coca leaves and Kola nut
A very fine, gentle wine formula
Pemberton's invention, immitation

First made by Angelo Marian
People loved the drink
Now unknown, a copy the only link

Sold for money to another
Many buyers, sons and brother
The fractions of stock divided

An ad in the paper, stock for sale
Three answered, Atlanta they moved
These medicines we'll send by mail

Atlanta druggist with a vision
With 2 others, controlled company
In exchange for debts owed

Pemberton grew ill, but still worked
A new drink he began to create
But died before it was done

The new company now owned by one
Chandler the wealthiest in Atlanta
The drink we all want now

Fire truck red, this is no joke
Ubiquitous sign , slogan we know
Things go better with coke

Neutral Spirit

Colorless, tasteless, scentless spirit
Unaged, neutral, distilled potato
Most made from anything that grows

Grain, barley, wheat, corn or rye
Dear little water, blends the beverage
Where it came from is still a question

A grand prince was told about Islam
It forbade alcohol or strong drink
Then he thought and Christian became

Wine sent by people from all around
Being a bit weak, it did not satisfy
Something stronger, the prince did cry

Even more sold by Ivan the Terrible
A network of distilleries and bars
This treasure given to future Tsärs

Absolutely no rivals allowed to sell
Except only those of Noble Blood
Served at banquets with church bells

Bread and vodka at formal meals
Peter the Great loved hospitality
Drink with friends, making a deal

Frozen during the winter months
A method for a stronger drink
When in this season, they did enter

Greater strength, more than once
Distillations, two or three times
Fermented liquid, turned to ice

First filtered sand, then river felt
Sometimes charcoal was used
Separation, the ice would melt

Clean aroma and spirit pure
Oily texture, light and high-proof
For years to come it will endure

Clear bottle on the shelf I see
Cold winters lasting long
Bottle hanging outside on a tree

Moonlight shone, glisten white
Floating waves, a winter night
To-fro, cold frosty winds bite

Footsteps I follow in the snow
Under the tree they stop, then go
Spears of icicles hanging low

As I look up into the tree high
I lose my balance on my back
Sounds of wind chimes cry

A sign you've drunk too much
Vodka frozen in the snow

On the shelf, not to touch...

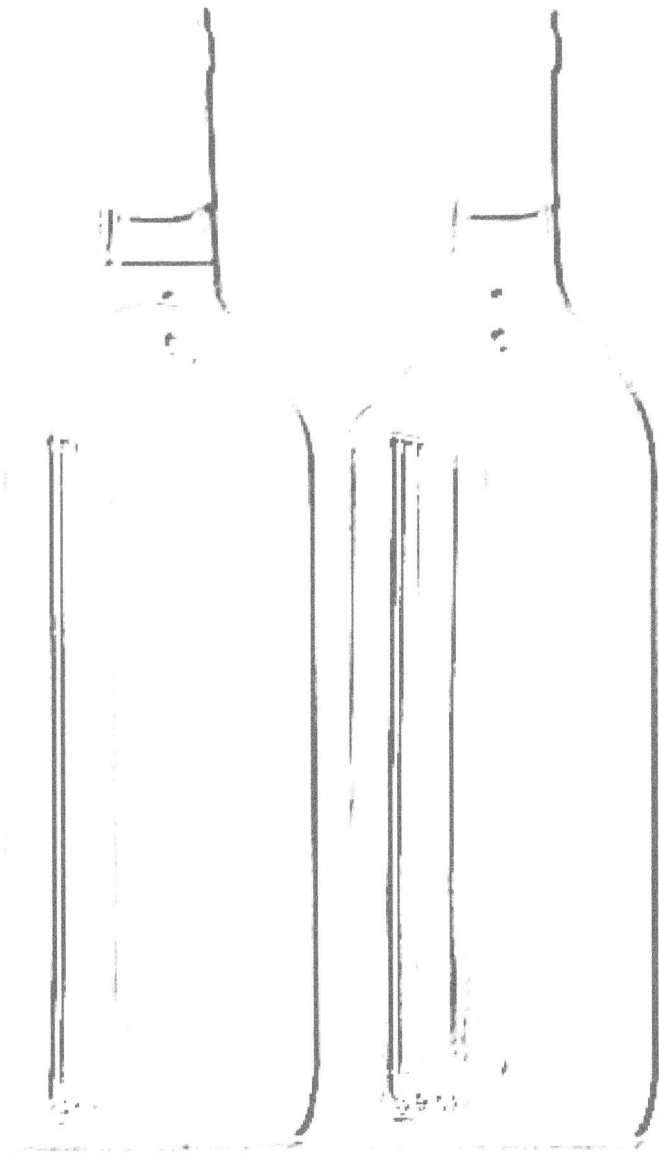

Mezcal-Tequila

A secret plant they could discover
Agave the flowering flower
Changed a man into a lover

The Spaniards call it Pulque
Cut before it can bloom
Let the plant ferment and lay

From agave the spirit produced
Not from cactus as they say
Since then many people seduced

In a small town in Mexico
The drink perfected even more
Tequila, Tequila... or Chinaco...

The only place it's made
Where blue agave grows
Ten years old to make the grade

The core, the pina, 100 pounds
Boiled for its honey juice
Gold, white and silver goose

Anejo aged for at least a year
Sometimes three or up to seven
Rest in oak until time is near

Premium mezcal produced outside
For true tequila "Anejo"

The bottom worm will hide

In the Mouth

Kuchikami sake was made
By everyone in the village
Chewing rice and chestnut

Into a tub they spat the juice
After some time, then mold
Ferment-mix-cook-wait...

Years later, a new method
More yield, was the decree
Now everywhere, far and wide

Seasons are hot and cold
Sake is served cold and hot
Room temperature, best I'm told

Tradition and rituals still today
Festivals, ceremonies, victory
Spread good fortune, iwai-zaki

Special rice called shinpaku-mai
The well known tamanohikari
Underground spring is nearby

With a dish, taste to savor
Mild and ideal companion
The country with the rising sun

Barrels and large bottles stay
Stacked up high for people to see
Drink too much, drop to your knee

From the Sky

Covering most of our planet
Constituting a portion of anatomy
Flowing and used freely
Ever changing form and constant
From gas to liquid or solid
Falling gracefully from the sky

Home to creatures some unknown
Of every shape and size
Even a place of fun as time flies
Mixed up with other elements
Harnessed to work, create energy
Washing our world and me

A glass of it I hold in my hand
Clear, no color, drops, tiny, and big...
Waves rolling with power to dig
The crystal ball of earth rotates
Wish to see the picture that's inside
Gently falling, taking me for a ride

Sounds that patter, floating dream
Nurturing life, falling from the sky
This place where grass is green

Bread and Man

From long ago and up to now
Everyday, every meal
Invented soon after the wheel

The scientists discover the baker
Sow and reap the ground
Turning millstone round and round

A stone-age cake they made
Communities began to swell
Near a stream or deep water well

Wandering and hunting stopped
Done now by only a few
Wild animals are kept in the zoo

At the start the machine spins
Make the selection that you like
A few hours later, out of the tin

On the table, left to cool a while
This bread aroma floats in the air
From wild grass and oats is where

In the bakery, they also sell
Loaves of different size and shape
Samples are served on a plate

Symbols of bread throughout history
Grow and harvest this precious grain

From fertile soil, sunshine and rain

Coffyns and Traps

Closed cover or open-top crust
A casserole, a party shell
Flour, butter, serve at the feast
Some meat or a fruit delight
Cookbook recipes began to appear
Apple, Chess, Chiffon, Crisps
Cobblers, Crumble, Buckle Grunts
Pandowdy, Pumpkin, Shoofly pie
Across the sea the pilgrims fly
Pioneers baked under the sky
Saved until the end of the meal
Gatherings, picnics, parties and fairs
Lifetime of history, a stomach big
Millionaires, writers, presidents, kings
Then, chefs creative crafts became
Sculptures, ornaments, a new name
Bigger and bigger, they grew and grew
Filled with blackbirds and people too
Sprinkled with sugar, then a surprise
Ideas, herbs, a spice, culinary hint
Greeks, Romans, Egyptians, Germans
Pastries, pies, history before our eyes
This a most pleasant sight to see
Steal a taste before others can try

Dance Greek-Eat Greek

Celebrate happiness, sweet sorrow
  In the company of family and friends
Close ties and some bridges to mend
  Or some important feast of the year
Special edibles, holidays and food
  Cooking permeates the cool fresh air
Decorated sweet Easter bread fair
  Magnificent dancing, bright flames
Migrating and returning home
  To over flowing baskets of fruit
It's waiting for me, my family too
  Cookies everywhere I see
Varvara for the neighbors
  December is the month
The feast of Saint Barbara
  Sprinkled fine with cinnamon
Through the shops and centuries
  Turkey, lamb, potatoes are sold
Christmas only once a year
  Inside the bread, always some gold
Five loaves to bless this day
  The unmarried girl takes to church
Then we dance, sing and eat

  Together... Share Joy and Greek

Essence of life

Passion for two thousand years
Apicius from Roman times
Cookbook of food and culture

Passed down and reconstructed
Found in the Vatican's library
Writers of recipes from the first

Cuisine not lost after the fall
Taken here and added there
First local, now varies worldwide

Food eaten through seasons
Parma, Polenta, Cheeses, Fruit
Ricotta, Mozzarella, Provolone

Sunshine glistens, red tomatoes
Yellow golden apple, Pomo D'Oro
A light, fluffy flat bread pie

On the coast, a medley of seafood
Mussels, baby clams, squid, octopus
Prawns, sardines, and red mullet

On the islands, roasted on a spit
Rich harvest of soy and stew
Sweet Cassata ice cream cake

Pasta of numerous shapes and sizes
Imaginative and diverse sauces
Delightful dining, humble or grandeur

Taste and Flavor

Food, land, cheek and tongue
Then the taste we know
Describe to others and agree

To smell and taste the flavor
Some say there are four
Chinese affirm, four and one more

Elements of the world we know
Water, fire, wood, metal, and earth
Five-spice powder, magic mixture

In the book of "Spring and Autumn"
A historical culinary masterpiece
Recipes recorded down with history

Seaweed sauce brings out five
In Japan it is called umami
Some tout a savory match for two

Now mass produced MSG
Study continues to this day
Musical notes and seven tastes

But not all, because one is bland
The other extra sweet
That leaves us with a pentatonic treat

Back and forth, tongue and cheek
Where taste and flavor number four
This is where the taste is square

To make this delicious and complete
One needs five-spice powder
Cast steel wok and some heat

One handle or two-handle pan
This choice is left up to you
Size, one yard or one foot round

Now with food there are names
Here are some for you to know
Grab your wok, onto the flames

Lions head meatballs
Ants climbing tree
Crossing the bridge noodles

Beggars chicken, a story told
Homeless along the road
Sighting a chicken alone

Now how to cook this food
Cover it with mud, to the fire it goes
Seductive aroma floating in the air

The Emperor happens to pass by
With the beggar, he eats a fine meal
Dine with an Emperor and nobility

With his court, share food and feel
Taste delicious noble chicken
Give thanks to bless the meal

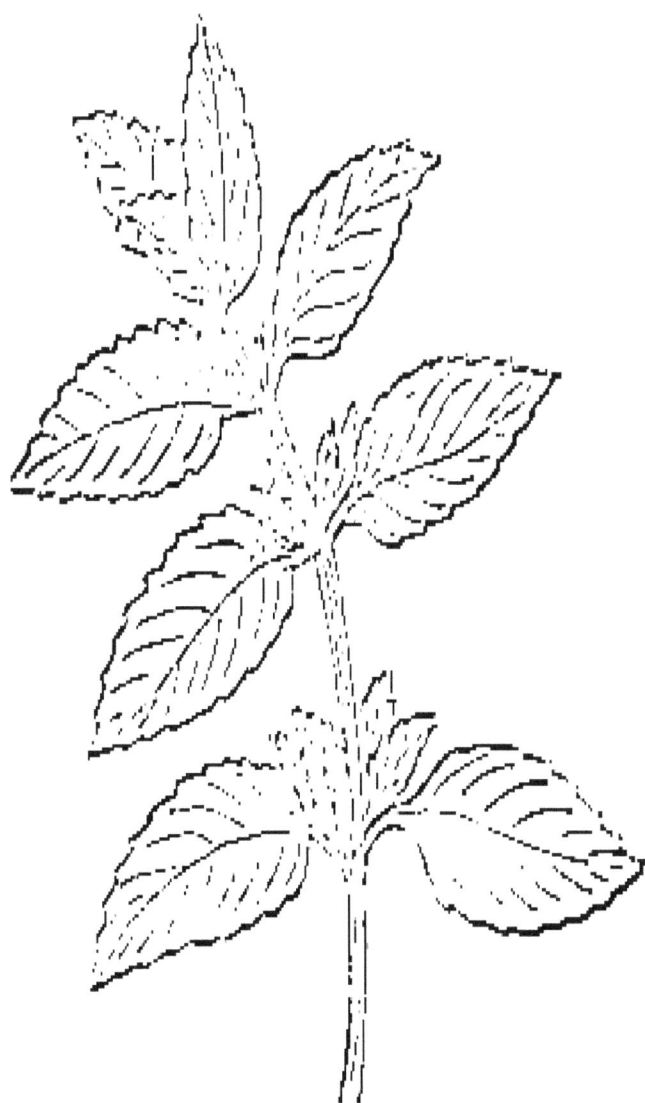

Across the Border

Rio Grande flows on by
Through canyons and land
Spanish conquest of the Aztec
Conquerors looking for gold
The real glory found in the food

The plant the Aztecs held sacred
Provided life and energy
Eaten raw, boiled or roasted
Stone-ground, corn gruel atole
Nixtamel, masa dough, tortillas

Small ball of masa, flattened thin
Tossed on the griddle, comal
After a minute, over once
The bread of Mexico today
Eaten just about any old way

Cortez looked for gold and fortune
A culinary treasure was found
Chocolate, peanut, vanilla, squash
Avocados, coconuts, tomatoes
And a simple way to cook...

The Spanish brought their delight
Pork, beef, lamb, citrus, garlic
Cheese, wheat, milk and wine
When they arrived, were given gold
Hunger for more was not a surprise

Many bloody battles were fought
Between Aztec and Spanish
Aztec culture still remains today
Emerging to an everlasting cuisine
Africa, Caribbean, French, Tex-Mex

Long before Europeans came
Olmecs, Huastecs, and Totonacs
Herbs named acayo, hoja stanta
Only beans, corn, squash and fruit
Meso American cooking root

Spaniards brought parsley, thyme
Bay laurel, cilantro, marjoram
Wheat, rice, almonds, red snapper
Caribbean pineapples, sugar cane
The region has never been the same

Quesadillas, a Mexican hybrid dish
Cajeta candy, rompope liqueur
French inspired walnut sauce
Poor folks and rich are patrons
North and south, more than one

Native foreign food, Tex-Mex
Only one place does it exist
Well-fried beans and chili
Fajita in the cantina
Burritos in the bar

Chimichanga, burrito fried far...
Toasted golden brown monkey
Creative invention or accident
Storied of wonder, simmer for a time
Christopher Columbus influence, 1492

Legends originate, warm valley dew
From Central America to Peru
Anise scented foliage, wild egg
Mole, tamales, and latin torta

Voyage the world, follow the wind

Mess Hall

Early in the morning
Men stand in a straight line
Waiting for their turn
One comes out, one goes in
Stand in line, "inside" again
Holding an empty tray
Fork, knife, napkin, spoon
Moving steadily along
Mess hall aroma all around
Beginning to froth, starving
Finally I can see the food
Order it fast, no turning back
Make up your mind, no time
I have my food, on my way
Looking for a table, a chair
There's one in sight...
Down I sit, dig in, eating fast
Not much talking, tired morning
No one cares, the time is tight
One goes out, one goes in
Everyday and tomorrow again
We are hungry, hard-working men
Buildings, windows and walls
All of them look the same to me

Except the one called the Mess Hall

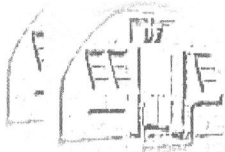

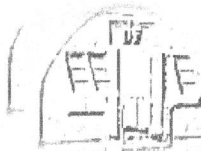

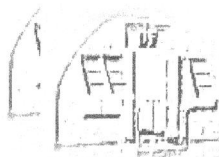

Renaissance and Revolution

From Roman self-indulgence
Rich, extravagant, magnificent
Gaul government by Roman law
The external city would grow
But the Roman Empire would fall

Five centuries of fine cookery
Gourmet, written Roman recipes
Practical food from many tribes
Copied by monks, still read today
Culinary advice for everyone's life

Lifestyle spent in the Middle Ages
Customs became close and familiar
Soldiers, merchants, and citizens
Enjoying pleasures from the table
De re coquinaria still adding pages

National passion for food and wine
A special region, variety of cuisine
The Loire valley, Saumur, Sologne
Gascogne, Perigord, Bayonne
Sweet...fresh... basil for pistou soup

For the French chef, the word fresh
All products for the Bistro new
Named specialties, original place
Varieties of fresh cheese, oysters
Cognac brandy or fine Bordeaux

Then the patisserie picnic
Tartines, Baguettes, croissants
Many possible shapes to see
Squares, pyramids, hearts, crottins
Chestnut leaves and cheese

We can't forget the essence of life
Wine a pleasure to enjoy
Everyone gives and freely offered
Vineyards, Loire Valley toast
German borders, Mediterranean

The best Reds and crystalline whites
Rules to follow, local food and wine
Whites first, then red when one dines
Culture and history in every drop
After one glass, it's hard to stop

A culinary art, no shortcuts
Mastery, preparation, careful
No helpful time-saving technique
If it's worth eating and cooking
Seek and it shall be found

Towns are well known, famous
Vegetables, cheeses or wine
Understood, known by the chef
Which is appropriate for mealtime
Cheese, meat, vegetable, red or white

An evolution of food to explore
No eating or cooking prohibitions
Seafood, poultry, or even fish
Culinary adventures and experience
To entertain, inform and investigate

Mother, grandmother learned
Habits and table setting order
What to eat first and then next
Middle ages, spanning history
Linked to legends and mystery

Medieval meal for a peasant
Firewood found and gathered
Remember a song, "Nine Days Old"
Pot of stew always on a burning fire
Cooking ever and never cold

Holiday chicken or other game
Perhaps a meat or stew frumenty
Habits of people, culture endure
Even today some are still pure
Unknown from where they came

Fresh, light, very clear flavor
Meat served rare or lightly cooked
Luxury, imagination still achieved
Constant, meticulous preparation
Not one small detail overlooked

Fruit-flavored vinegar seasoning
Renaissance the last fifty years
Spices obtained from the orient far
A new creation and class became
Brilliant, glowing, shining star

Europeans change their taste
How they lived, dressed and ate
A huge variety of food on display
All sitting, choose from a buffet
Discussion at the table, hours late

Centuries later and revolution
Gastronomy recorded in France
French identity, language and food
Reach for what one wants to eat
The Russian style became ideal

Have your meal in one course
Eat your meal, choose one dish
Dining chaos changed to order
Eat and dine the royal style
Portions or plates or what you wish

Across generations, cooking judged
Worldwide market widens its range
This food, this wine, this time...
Many have the chance, experience...

Cross the bridge, dine royally

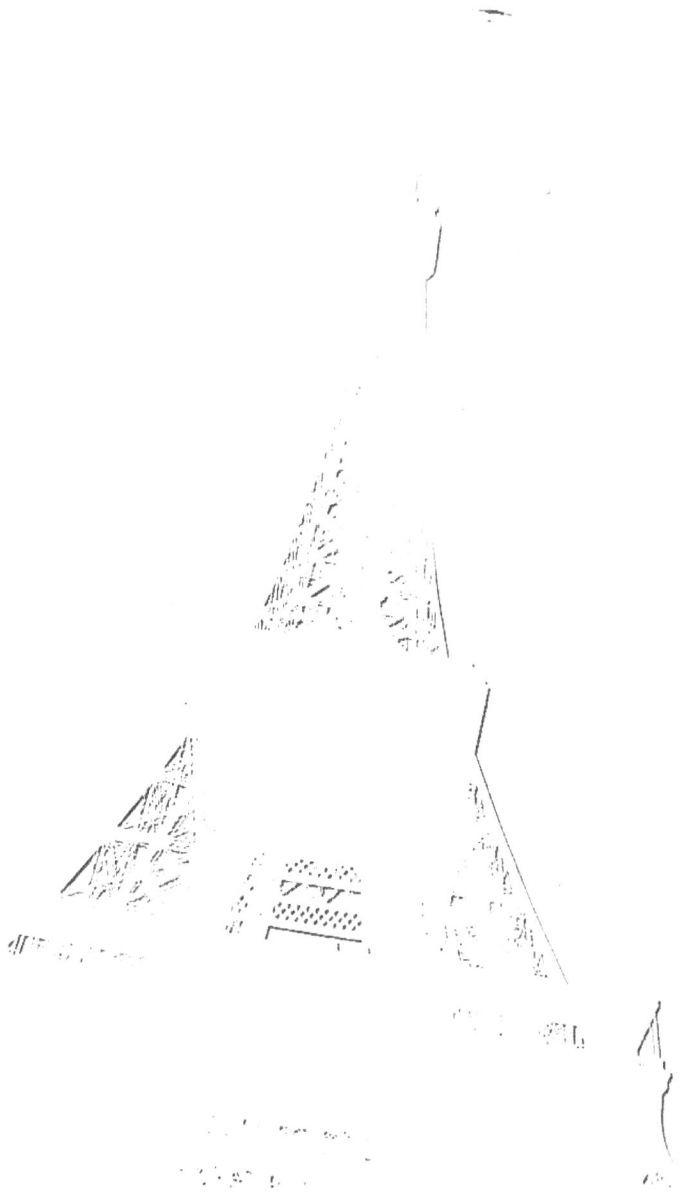

Hunters-Fishers-Gatherers

Four chief islands, many more small
Volcanic, precipitous, heavy rainfall
Fish and rice abundant, no red meat
Twelve hundred years was this rule
Five flavors, five colors for food

Joman, a period long ago in time
Then the Yayoi, a migrating tribe
Iron, pottery, wine, creative ideas
Yamamoto, Soga, clans of power
Military class strong, called Samurai

Kofun time, and a fertile plain
Land bought by the government
Let the farmers grow their crops
Food is plenty, a simple visual fashion
Most important, on the table, in sight

A menu of delight, alluring, charming
Two-thousand year, rice bowl feast
Uniform, plain, unison, the same
Breakfast and then at every meal
Boiled or cooked on a charcoal grill

Used for everything, paper to food
Rice, mixed or eaten from a bowl
Variety add or your own free choice
Sushi, Sashimi, round - round it goes
Also the color of the chopsticks count

From the north, highlands in Hokkaido
To the south, warm islands in Okinawa
Cooking style change, coming around
Noodles hot, noodles cold, noodles sold
Yakitori chicken on skewer or stick

Onigiri, rice in nori, seaweed wrap
Ramen noodles, travel from China
Old style nabe, hot, potluck soup
Natural harmony, never kill the taste
Food and person, a very small group

Question, how often to eat the rice
Everyday for two thousand years
Value paid as money, tax and wage
Mochi rice cake, hot miso soup
Now in this season, what do we eat?

Bamboo shoots-chestnuts-mushrooms
Observe and enjoy with your eyes
Aesthetic sense, create food as art
Blue chopsticks, green maple leaf
Tea, beer, sake, "itadakemus"

"I am going to eat now"

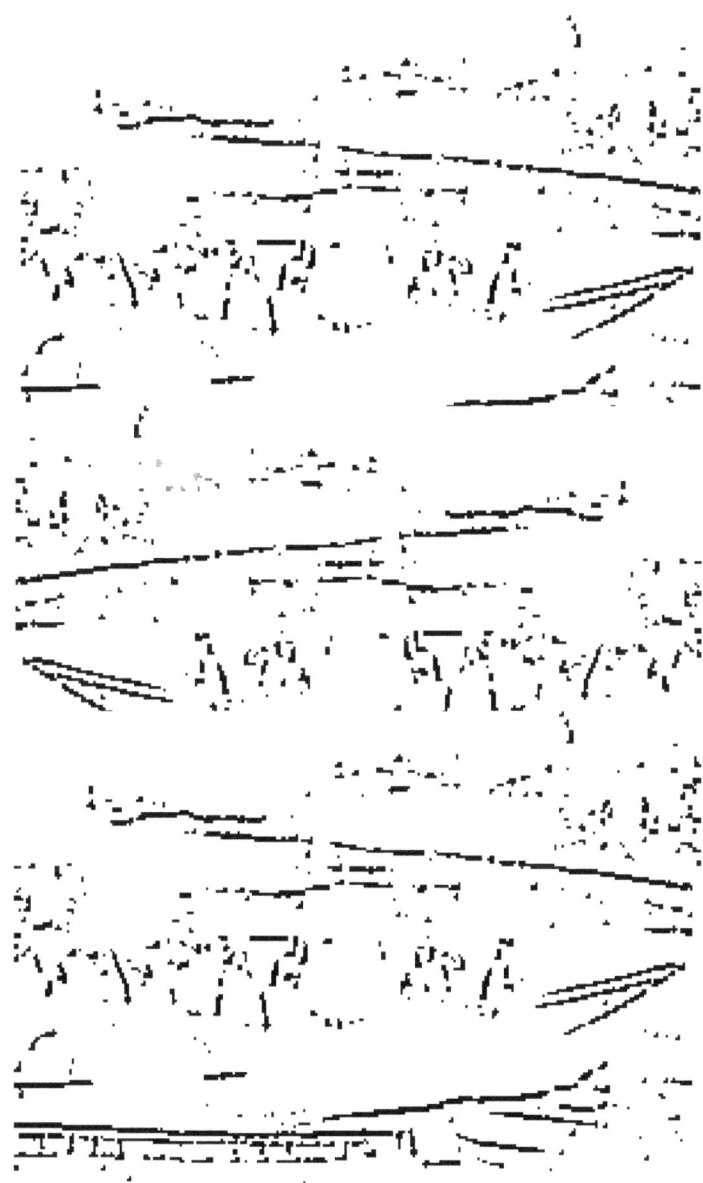

My New Friends

One young traveling adventurer
Broken down car began to walk

Tent at night, wayside wandering

Hunger never leaves or goes away
This is Texas, a big, big place

Looking for some work and food

A camper park up the road
One family having dinner alone

At a table I sit with no food

Drinking water from a fountain
Water for dinner, all I can afford

Suddenly silently, without a word...

A dish is placed in front of me
There's nothing said, only a smile

Then gone away, eat like a king

Meat, rice, chicken, Mexican treat
Under the glow of a street light

Savor every bite and morsel delight

My stomach full, feeling satisfied
No one here or in my sight

Sounds of traffic pass slowly by

I rest my head, hand upright
Night's image revolves around me

True painting of life, open eyes

Surprise!

Reach

Up from the restraining earth
Slowly thriving, rising upward
Digesting and absorbing life
Growing to an unlimited sky
Importing vitality all around
Deeply rooted, secret not found

A portion down in the earth
Green spreading over the ground
Picked from a plant or a tree
This perishable tender life
I clutch in my engaging hand
Still alive, ridged, solid, strong

Soon the life will pass
From this magnificent fragrance
Decompose, crumble and perish
Time is of most importance
Hunger can save one
No time to cook, eat it raw

Energy for me to grow
Vigor, I can be master
The last word, dominance

Hospitality Habit

Diverse people and cuisine
A spectrum of dietary extremes
Vegetarianism, meat-eating history

Vedic time, animals to appease
Sacrifice, the meat then eaten
New religion, the end of a trend

Preaching principle of Ahimsa
Not to harm or eat any meat
This doctrine called Atherrareda

To harm the deified cow, now a sin
Vegetarianism embraced by many
It's now a diet to stay thin, in shape

The animal a greater asset for us
It's better for it to stay alive
Milk, cheese, butter, yogurt

Sattuik, eating only vegetables
Spread from the north and beyond
Clear mind, pure long, thought long

A few eat mutton or some fish
Exchanged on the crossroads
Local cuisine's traveled far

Gastronomic revolution and spices
A little garnish, rice and meat
Kebabs and pilafs, sweetbreads

Scented water, end with dessert
Lavish meal on silver, porcelain
Royal families, court banquets

Naans, chapatis, diversity in bread
Fine white cloth spread over a floor
Customary to eat with fingers

A healthy meal is had by all
Friend and countrymen hear the call
Hospitality extended to all guests

Now in many ways and major cities
This food is enjoyed by all alike
Part of culture, life and atmosphere

Invitations sent out, please enjoy
Together we talk and exchange ideas

Passion of life, gift of friendship

91

Yankee Noodle

Originally Eastern Mediterranean
Made from many foodstuffs
Now present around the world

China's noodle history is clear
Adopted by the people quickly
Becoming the country's cuisine

Noodle know how found its way
Everywhere rice and wheat flourish
So there a noodle can be produced

Popular for longevity and nutrition
Easily stored, eaten hot or cold
Taken and transported anywhere

In Chinese"Lau Mein", boiled noodles
To Japan's north Hokkaido island
Around to Singapore, "Maggi Mee"

International food in many countries
Thick and thin, many kinds of flavors
Pleasing taste for all of us to savor

New macaroni pasta machines
Thomas Jefferson designed one too
Pride and glory, pasta my son

Tangled history, myth of the past
Down in the bowl, twisted vast
So easy to make, a comfort to eat

Hammering out noodles from dough
Beads that trap Venus and Mars
Left in the night above glowing stars

Evidence about Greek and Roman
Flattened dough, broad "Laganon"
Roasted on stones, eat from the pan

Kinsman to what we call pizza today
Enclosed timballi and a few pies
Layer of seasons, a covered surprised

Talmud in Aramaic, a noodle record
Itriyah vende, bought and dried
Some homemade, fresh when tried!

Flour-based staple, shapes and strings
Kneaded with feet, one whole day
Raisins, spices, golden sun ray

Sauces a question, still to this day
Italy provides a perfect climate
Semolina, hard wheat, futes lay

Maccaruni dough, made by force
From China or to China, on land, ship
Striking everywhere, crack the whip

Ippolito, a red tomato, delicious recipe
For meat, chicken, veal, with a fork
Manners and history, pop the cork

Nobel Prize winners, collected talent
Heads of state with political power
Extraordinary minds, together dine

Yankee Dutch, English doodle
With a feather sticking out of a hat
Famous pinstripes, baseball bat

Revolution, valiant fighting men
Singing songs, Battle for Bunker Hill
Quest for freedom, send me the bill

Joyful, spread the pasta everywhere
Kneaded dough by the baker's feet
Noodles made from pounded wheat

Naples, the modern noodle center
And the climates fair, pure, right...
American civil war at its height

Italians head for the New World
With them came the food they ate
Now a favorite dish on our plate

Ovid's Metamorphoses, sun, light
Venus and Mars together spent
Eternity and forever they went

A charming, vernal island continent
Excellent place for durum to grow
Wide-open spaces, where ideas flow

Fungus Plant

Vegetable growing, alive...
Oddity, no roots, flowers, seeds, leaves
Complex, poisonous and edible

Maturing wild, for everyone free
Some farmed, controlled market
Exotic, supplying this living fungus

Kennett Square, Pennsylvania place
American mushroom-producing grace
Exporting, supplying this lovely fungus

Shooting stems, plump not wrinkled
White, tan or creamy color
As they age, darker shades appear

Tasting stronger, more intense
Dry, fragile, carefully handled
Portobello, shiitake, firm and meaty

Special woodsy, outdoor smell
Soaking up odors like a sponge
Eaten fresh, rarely frozen

Off with the debris gently
Paper towel, soft clean brush
Mildly, softly, a mother's touch

With some, stems are food
Caps sometimes filled or stuffed
Crab, sausage, scallion, herb

Crimini, called Itailan Brown
Deeper color, like the ground
Wild mushroom, sold in town

Portobello are kings and giants
Six-inch diameter, gills repleat
Vegetarians eat them like meat

Enoki, pure white snow fan
Grow in and come from Japan
Sweet for salad, soup or raw

Oyster, some say phoenix shell
Thick and soft, a little chewy bell
Brown, white, pink or yellow

Shiitake, golden oak, Black Forest
Out in the wild, growing on logs
In Japan, a thousand years long

Chanterells, trumpets, umbrellas
Inside out, yellow reddish orange
Pepper nuts, exotic and wild

Horn of plenty, hen of the woods
Battering trumpet of lasting death
Chicken flavors on hardwood stumps

Hedgehog, Porcino or called Cepes
Boletus family, caps, standard gills
Thick, spongy, meaty, stuff and grill

Truffels, delicious delicacy, expensive
Hard to harvest, grown underground
Gommet, four hundred per pound

Morel, honeycombed, hollow brown
Earthy, with dark smokey flavor
Farm picked, wholesome fresh labor

A Cool Cucumber

Thank you Christopher Columbus
We are still eating your green gift
Planted on the Far Eastern coast
Florida's weather, they sell most

Loaded with water, high content
Crisp, moist, always cooler inside
Dark green color, firm and stout
A pleasant shape, not too large

Huge is bitter, bumps okay
Withered, shriveled, stay away
Wax for an extended life
Don't wash until you are ready

Leftovers in a bag, once a week
Eat with cheese, Italian or Greek
Skin on or skin off, your choice
Dill and mint, sautéed in butter

Garnish a Bloody Mary or salad
Varieties for slicing and picking
Flavors change, bitter or sour
They are garden leaves that flower

99

Strong and powerful

Found growing on the land
So since the city has been called
Shegaugawinshe is the name
Chicago and onion are the same

Powerful taste and stray aroma
The windy city, legend link
Planted early spring or late
Of Chicago, this we think

Eaten raw, just like an apple
Mild winter or summer days
Hot and sweet, shed a bitter tear
Peel the skin, around the maze

Gold, copper, red or white
Traditional cooking ingredient
Stings the tongue when one bites
Lightning strikes the flying kite

Hanging outside around a window
Seen as I walk past the house
Waving in the air, dancing slowly
Strong and powerful, almost holy

Herb

Diversity, select what's in sight
No spots or insect bite

Examined for freshness, aroma
Add some flavor, do re me fa

Don't wait too long, until limp
A glass or vase, frozen hard

Decoration, garnish, presentation
Ice cubes of herbs, that next dish

Parsley, licorice, anise mix
Seeds ground, flavor the pastries

Peppery arugula olive oil
Basil, clove, pungent leaf

Dull, green bay leaves, aromatic
Soups, stews, sauces, spaghetti

Chervil chopped for stew
Chives sprinkled over mushroom

Cilantro seafood, Indian salad
Dill for a pickle jar or barrel

Lemon grass peeled, undressed
Horseradish for a mustard test

Marjoram eggs, soups or lamb
Mint for drinks, sold we cheer

Oregano, all season, all food
Rosemary fragrant, aroma mood

Sage pebble leaf, mild strength
Sorrel, tarragon, a dash of thyme

Sunflower faces the sunshine
This is what makes us smile

Vitamin Link

Abundant, key, taken for granted
Sold on the street, this citrus crop

W. Wiltskill planted the first tree
Said, "I don't care if you laugh at me"

1849, the gold-rush miner
Customer with abundant cash

Some thought it was a fluke
The railroad built, St. Louis dash

California citrus, business is good
Eliza Tibbets had three branches

One of three, still alive today
Bearing fruit, while we play

California, Florida, the Mediterranean
Tropical, semi-tropical, oranges grow

Maturing quickly, color change is slow
Cool evenings, sunset, rainbow stream

Brazil number one, U.S. number two
Washington Naval, Seville of Spain

Blood red orange of Italy grows
Clementine of Morocco, Jaffe Israel

Large naval oranges are picked late
Best in a cool place to wait

Valencias yellow, orange then green
With cinnamon, mint triple sec

Dramatic look, upside down, all around
North, South, East and West

A section or slice, pith is found
Special vitamin, fills life with zest

On My List

Delicious sunset delight
Soft...silky...smooth to touch
Sweet and juicy, replete of flavor
Meaty texture, one is enough
Freestone, clingstone choose
Spring crest, germ-free season
Elegant land, O' Henry then
Supermarkets filled, gardens tend
Fragrance blush, soft and firm
Yielding to a gentle, soothing caress
Douse with cool, flowing freshwater
In one's hand, roll, turn, and tumble
Serve with poultry, chosen course
Veal, rum, amaretto this drink
Slice or two with red wine
Fabulous dessert made very fine
June lady, spring lady, rich lady
Yellow red blaze, spring crest
White seed arrives, full of life
Georgia peach, to be my wife
Well-matured, truly ripened glow
Fair time frozen, harvest show
Exceptional this category twist
Always on my shopping list

One a Day

Throughout the world they're grown
Delicious is sweet and crisp
Gala and Fuji seed are blown
Applesauce, juice, jellies ensue
Cold trigger, cycle begins
Season spring and flowers
Bud and grow from April showers
Cool autumn harvest crop
Other names you may not know
Granny Smith, bright green tart
Golden Delicious, yellow freckles
Rome glossy red, cooking begins
Macintosh, tender fine eating
Jonathan from New York
Gravenstein stripped unique
Staymans purplish pouring juice
Imperial firm, baking again
Empire, the all purpose jack
Spy gold bits of other grades
Kiwi apple, cold stays fresh
A bad apple will spoil the rest
For a long healthy life...
One a day, is the best!

For the Chef

Year 'round appearance, all at once
Hand-picked, peaceful, still green
Seldom eaten alone, always a brace
Wet climates echo, recite farewell

In drinks or on food, it's applied
Chicken, fish, salad, or clams
Bloody Marys, martinis a twist
Pie or ham, bright peel, heavy size

Accent for a meal, counting weeks
Squeeze for juice, buy a bottle
Wash, dry and cut for later
Zest can be a treat to cater

Room temperature for two weeks
Refrigerate longer, freeze to keep
Green thumb, the gardeners reap
Limetlas, a sweet luscious hybrid

Eurekas, full of seeds to clean
Lisbons, smooth-watery-regale
Serve to friends and guests
For the chef, Meyer fills the need

Ruby Red

Two thousand years back or more
Straw was spread under the berries
On this straw carried to market
Sold to merchants to profit merry

Wild forest, fragrant as a rose
Romans found this cousin there
Europeans traveled to America
Found strawberries under their toes

Cultivated and sent to England
The flavor loved by everyone
A white strawberry from Chile
Marry, growing under the sun

The fruit with seeds outside
Unique plant, the only one
This sensation, a sweet berry
Pick then eat, while others carry

California coast, perfect climate
Ripen as they lay in one's hand
Breakfast, lunch, dessert we eat
Always enjoyable, ruby red treat

110

Queen of Hearts

Sold on a sunny afternoon roadside
Picnics, fireworks, holiday fun
Parade of cars, all in a row
The watermelon star of the show

Firm symmetrical, no cuts or dents
The rind is hard, an appealing sheen
Can it be eaten? We need a test
Just give a thump to the green

Almost all water and very heavy
Room temperature and a little time
Slice, serve and take a bite
A treat anytime, day or night

Twist of the wrist, smooth as silk
Viking boat of unique green
Round lemon shields all around
Carved and shaped with style

Centerpiece, jubilee sweet
Peacock, calsweet yellow, icebox
Desert king, Queen of hearts
Dissimilar name from the same part

Fuzzy Brown

Vines like shrubs growing tall
One thousand years in all
This berry grows on trees
Hayward Wright heard the call

Egg-shaped fuzzy brown skin
Three inches long, come along
Black seeds that are good to eat
Just peel the paper-thin skin

From California to New Zealand
Grown and eaten all year round
Plump, full of flavor, ripe to touch
Bought at a roadside stand

Room temperature for a week
In a hurry, grab a paper bag
Some ethylene banana gas
After a week, take a quick glance

Bright green scoop with a spoon
Slice into pieces with a knife
Peel and rub, draw the fuzz
On a sunny day or under the moon

Flying Pineapple

Fruit a plant, pineapple sweet
Hawaii, Australia, South America
Royal family, China maw is king
Everywhere enjoying the ripening

Transplanted around the world
Under Portuguese and Spanish wing
Improved by trial and weather
Fresh, deep, clean, green leaves

Harvest at the right moment
Not too green, not too ripe
Sweetness chosen, then eat
Magical note, gisten and shine

Placed on a table to welcome
A gift for me they bring
Tropical aroma floats above
This completes the atmosphere

Feeling dry, count round gilt rings
Cayenne, Champaka, Del Monte Gold
Red Spanish Queen, Permambuco
Up from the ground, this gold springs

Hunger & Thirst

From inside the feeling runs
Aroma has a significant role
And what about the time of day
How hard one works or energy play

On the field, hard fought game
Almost any sport, rough or tame
A trophy for the champion today
Feast for the fans, coaches and players

Back-breaking, digging, wrenching, toil
Covered with the smell, sweat and soil
Waiting for a... or the... bell to ring...
Freedom, celebrate the end of the day

To home, protective comfortable nest
Left over, fresh or familiar fare
A night on the town, east and west
Late night, early morning, tired day

Perhaps gastronomic, what's in view
Choices are made from a menu
Friends tell me what is best
From an experiment, the true test

Tastes range from person to person
Growing change, time continues to pass
Scratching my head in amazment
Broken rules are somewhat bent

Crumbs for some, how dare one
Parched lips, a drop to soothe
Plenty searched for, never found
Harvest from the rich warm ground

Hunger filled, thirst refreshed, spirit raised
Some indulge with a dessert so sweet
With life a meal taken everyday...
Common, regular, or chance a gift pay

Survival no choice, just to bear
Without power, give in to force
Dry, moist, changing with the weather
Bones and muscle diminish and tear

Mercy, forgivness, some air... light...
From where does the food then fall?
Outstretched arms, hands of plenty...
Mouths clamor to moan at the wall

Pofad

Through the streets, a slow pace
Aroma floats closely by
Endless choice on my mind
Voices calling, singing brightly

Pleasure, experience, atmosphere
Some people sitting here and there
A menu of words, hard and heavy
Description painted in front of me

Great selection, open to see
Soon the decision must be made
Stepping stone found in the road
All for me or perhaps to share

Brought, given, service kind
Before me waiting, it does lie
Remember manner, style and grace
Exchange, equal trade

Apocope

Up along the trellis
No longer touching earth
A cheerful crawling vine

Twisting all around
Every which way and that
This color of pine

Destination unknown
Ornamental tangle of ribbon
Shift course, new virgin line

Hunting sunlight and rain
Roots grow robust
Leaves bluster and shine

Climate a struggle
What yield to come?
We pray it be fine

Harvest stage, amine
Interlude for the throng
Celebrating bounty, rejoice

Jubilee... Drink sweet wine...

117

Bon
Appetit

www.ingramcontent.com/pod-product-compliance
Lightning Source LLC
Chambersburg PA
CBHW061745020426
42331CB00006B/1356